50 Cooking with Seasonal Berries

By: Kelly Johnson

Table of Contents

- Strawberry Lemonade Muffins
- Blueberry Pancake Soufflé
- Raspberry Glazed Salmon
- Blackberry Goat Cheese Tart
- Mixed Berry Chia Pudding
- Cranberry Pecan Scones
- Strawberry Basil Bruschetta
- Blueberry Almond Smoothie Bowl
- Raspberry Vanilla Cheesecake Bars
- Blackberry Mint Iced Tea
- Cranberry Orange Relish
- Strawberry Shortcake Trifle
- Blueberry BBQ Chicken Skewers
- Raspberry Rose Sorbet
- Blackberry Lemon Curd Tartlets
- Mixed Berry Spinach Salad
- Cranberry Apple Stuffing
- Strawberry Chocolate Chip Cookies
- Blueberry Honey Glazed Pork Chops
- Raspberry Swirl Ice Cream
- Blackberry Sage Gravy
- Mixed Berry Pavlova
- Cranberry Ginger Cocktail
- Strawberry Ricotta Pancakes
- Blueberry Lemon Yogurt Cake
- Raspberry Almond Crumb Bars
- Blackberry Jalapeño Jam
- Mixed Berry Oat Bars
- Cranberry Bourbon Glazed Ham
- Strawberry Kiwi Popsicles
- Blueberry Balsamic Chicken Salad
- Raspberry Chocolate Lava Cakes
- Blackberry Vanilla Bean Panna Cotta
- Mixed Berry Quinoa Salad
- Cranberry Almond Energy Balls

- Strawberry Lavender Mocktail
- Blueberry Coconut Ice Cream
- Raspberry Hazelnut Tart
- Blackberry Thyme Roasted Vegetables
- Mixed Berry Breakfast Parfait
- Cranberry Glazed Meatballs
- Strawberry Rosewater Macarons
- Blueberry Lemonade
- Raspberry Brie Puff Pastry
- Blackberry Bourbon Smash
- Mixed Berry Cobbler
- Cranberry Chocolate Bark
- Strawberry Mango Salsa
- Blueberry Protein Pancakes
- Raspberry Lime Mousse

Strawberry Lemonade Muffins

Ingredients

- **For the Muffins:**
    - 1 ¾ cups (220g) all-purpose flour
    - 1 tsp baking powder
    - ½ tsp baking soda
    - ¼ tsp salt
    - ½ cup (115g) unsalted butter, softened
    - ¾ cup (150g) granulated sugar
    - 2 large eggs
    - ⅓ cup (80ml) fresh lemon juice (about 1-2 lemons)
    - Zest of 1 lemon
    - ½ cup (120ml) plain yogurt or sour cream
    - 1 cup (150g) fresh strawberries, diced
- **For the Lemon Glaze:**
    - 1 cup (120g) powdered sugar
    - 2-3 tbsp fresh lemon juice

Instructions

1. **Preheat Oven:**
   Preheat your oven to 375°F (190°C). Line a 12-cup muffin tin with paper liners or grease the tin.
2. **Prepare Dry Ingredients:**
   In a medium bowl, whisk together the flour, baking powder, baking soda, and salt. Set aside.
3. **Cream Butter and Sugar:**
   In a large mixing bowl, use a hand mixer or stand mixer to cream together the butter and sugar until light and fluffy (about 2 minutes).
4. **Add Wet Ingredients:**
   Beat in the eggs one at a time, then mix in the lemon juice, lemon zest, and yogurt until smooth.
5. **Combine Wet and Dry Ingredients:**
   Gradually fold the dry ingredients into the wet mixture. Do not overmix. Gently fold in the diced strawberries.
6. **Fill Muffin Tin:**
   Divide the batter evenly among the prepared muffin cups, filling each about ¾ full.

7. **Bake:**
   Bake for 18-22 minutes, or until a toothpick inserted into the center of a muffin comes out clean.
8. **Cool:**
   Allow the muffins to cool in the pan for 5 minutes before transferring them to a wire rack to cool completely.
9. **Prepare Lemon Glaze:**
   In a small bowl, whisk together the powdered sugar and lemon juice until smooth. Drizzle over the cooled muffins.
10. **Serve:**
    Enjoy your muffins fresh or store them in an airtight container at room temperature for up to 2 days.

Blueberry Pancake Soufflé

Ingredients:

- 1 cup fresh blueberries
- 2 tbsp granulated sugar
- 4 large eggs, separated
- 1 cup buttermilk
- 1 tsp vanilla extract
- 1 cup all-purpose flour
- 2 tbsp unsalted butter, melted
- 1 tsp baking powder
- ¼ tsp salt
- Powdered sugar, for dusting

Instructions:

1. Preheat the oven to 375°F (190°C). Grease a 9-inch round baking dish.
2. In a small bowl, mix blueberries with 1 tbsp sugar. Set aside.
3. In a large bowl, whisk egg yolks, buttermilk, vanilla extract, flour, melted butter, baking powder, and salt until smooth.
4. In another bowl, beat the egg whites until soft peaks form. Gradually add the remaining 1 tbsp sugar and continue to beat until stiff peaks form.
5. Gently fold the egg whites into the batter, then fold in the blueberries.
6. Pour the batter into the prepared baking dish. Bake for 25-30 minutes, or until puffed and golden brown.
7. Dust with powdered sugar before serving. Enjoy immediately!

Raspberry Glazed Salmon

Ingredients:

- 4 salmon fillets
- 1 cup fresh raspberries
- 2 tbsp honey
- 1 tbsp balsamic vinegar
- 1 tbsp Dijon mustard
- Salt and pepper, to taste
- 1 tbsp olive oil

Instructions:

1. Preheat the oven to 400°F (200°C).
2. In a small saucepan, combine raspberries, honey, balsamic vinegar, Dijon mustard, salt, and pepper. Simmer over medium heat for 5-7 minutes, or until raspberries break down and sauce thickens.
3. Season the salmon fillets with salt and pepper. Heat olive oil in a skillet over medium-high heat. Cook the salmon for 3-4 minutes per side, or until golden brown.
4. Brush the raspberry glaze over the salmon fillets during the last 2 minutes of cooking.
5. Serve the salmon with extra raspberry glaze and garnish with fresh raspberries.

Blackberry Goat Cheese Tart

Ingredients:

- 1 pre-made tart crust (or homemade)
- 8 oz goat cheese, softened
- 1/2 cup heavy cream
- 2 tbsp honey
- 1 tsp vanilla extract
- 1 cup blackberries
- Fresh mint leaves, for garnish

Instructions:

1. Preheat the oven to 350°F (175°C). Bake the tart crust according to package instructions, if using a pre-made crust.
2. In a bowl, combine the goat cheese, heavy cream, honey, and vanilla extract. Beat until smooth and creamy.
3. Spread the goat cheese mixture evenly over the cooled tart crust.
4. Arrange the blackberries on top of the goat cheese filling.
5. Bake the tart for 10-12 minutes, or until the edges of the crust are golden.
6. Let the tart cool before garnishing with fresh mint leaves. Slice and serve chilled or at room temperature.

Mixed Berry Chia Pudding

Ingredients:

- 1 cup mixed berries (blueberries, strawberries, raspberries)
- 2 cups almond milk (or any milk of choice)
- 3 tbsp chia seeds
- 1 tbsp maple syrup (optional)
- 1 tsp vanilla extract

Instructions:

1. In a blender, combine the mixed berries, almond milk, maple syrup, and vanilla extract. Blend until smooth.
2. Pour the mixture into a bowl and stir in the chia seeds.
3. Cover and refrigerate for at least 4 hours or overnight, allowing the chia seeds to absorb the liquid and thicken.
4. Before serving, stir the pudding and top with extra fresh berries or a drizzle of honey.

Cranberry Pecan Scones

Ingredients:

- 2 cups all-purpose flour
- 1 tbsp baking powder
- ½ tsp salt
- ½ cup cold unsalted butter, cubed
- ⅓ cup sugar
- 1 large egg
- ½ cup heavy cream
- 1 tsp vanilla extract
- 1 cup fresh cranberries
- ½ cup chopped pecans

Instructions:

1. Preheat your oven to 400°F (200°C). Line a baking sheet with parchment paper.
2. In a large bowl, whisk together the flour, baking powder, salt, and sugar.
3. Cut in the butter using a pastry cutter or your hands until the mixture resembles coarse crumbs.
4. Add the egg, cream, and vanilla extract. Stir until just combined.
5. Gently fold in the cranberries and pecans.
6. Turn the dough out onto a floured surface and pat into a circle. Cut into 8 wedges and place on the baking sheet.
7. Bake for 15-18 minutes, or until golden brown. Cool on a wire rack.

Strawberry Basil Bruschetta

Ingredients:

- 1 pint fresh strawberries, diced
- ¼ cup fresh basil, chopped
- 1 tbsp balsamic vinegar
- 1 tsp honey
- 1 loaf baguette, sliced
- Olive oil for brushing

Instructions:

1. Preheat the oven to 375°F (190°C).
2. Brush the baguette slices with olive oil and toast them on a baking sheet for about 5-7 minutes, or until golden.
3. In a bowl, combine the diced strawberries, basil, balsamic vinegar, and honey. Stir to combine.
4. Spoon the strawberry mixture onto the toasted baguette slices and serve immediately.

Blueberry Almond Smoothie Bowl

Ingredients:

- 1 cup frozen blueberries
- 1 banana
- ½ cup almond milk (or any milk of choice)
- 2 tbsp almond butter
- 1 tbsp chia seeds
- Granola and fresh berries for topping

Instructions:

1. In a blender, combine the frozen blueberries, banana, almond milk, and almond butter. Blend until smooth.
2. Pour into a bowl and top with granola, chia seeds, and fresh berries.
3. Enjoy immediately!

Raspberry Vanilla Cheesecake Bars

Ingredients:

- 1 ½ cups graham cracker crumbs
- ¼ cup sugar
- ⅓ cup melted butter
- 2 cups cream cheese, softened
- ¾ cup sugar
- 2 large eggs
- 1 tsp vanilla extract
- 1 cup fresh raspberries

Instructions:

1. Preheat the oven to 325°F (160°C). Line an 8x8-inch baking pan with parchment paper.
2. In a small bowl, mix the graham cracker crumbs, sugar, and melted butter. Press the mixture into the bottom of the prepared pan.
3. In a large bowl, beat the cream cheese and sugar until smooth. Add the eggs, one at a time, followed by the vanilla extract.
4. Pour the cheesecake batter over the crust and gently drop spoonfuls of raspberries on top.
5. Bake for 35-40 minutes, or until the center is set. Cool completely and refrigerate for at least 2 hours before serving.

Blackberry Mint Iced Tea

Ingredients:

- 4 cups water
- 4 black tea bags
- 1 cup fresh blackberries
- 2 tbsp fresh mint leaves
- 2 tbsp honey or sweetener of choice
- Ice cubes

Instructions:

1. Bring the water to a boil. Remove from heat and steep the tea bags for 5 minutes.
2. While the tea cools, muddle the blackberries and mint leaves in a pitcher.
3. Once the tea has cooled, pour it over the muddled berries and mint. Stir in the honey.
4. Refrigerate until chilled, then serve over ice.

Cranberry Orange Relish

Ingredients:

- 12 oz fresh cranberries
- 1 orange, peeled and chopped
- 1 cup sugar
- ½ cup water

Instructions:

1. In a saucepan, combine cranberries, orange, sugar, and water.
2. Bring to a simmer over medium heat and cook for 10-12 minutes, or until the cranberries burst and the mixture thickens.
3. Let cool and refrigerate until ready to serve.

Strawberry Shortcake Trifle

Ingredients:

- 1 pound fresh strawberries, sliced
- 1 tbsp sugar
- 1 pound sponge cake or pound cake, cut into cubes
- 2 cups heavy whipping cream
- ¼ cup powdered sugar
- 1 tsp vanilla extract

Instructions:

1. Toss the sliced strawberries with sugar and let them sit for 10 minutes.
2. In a large bowl, whip the heavy cream, powdered sugar, and vanilla extract until stiff peaks form.
3. In a large trifle dish, layer the cake cubes, whipped cream, and strawberries. Repeat the layers until the dish is full.
4. Refrigerate for at least 2 hours before serving.

Blueberry BBQ Chicken Skewers

Ingredients:

- 2 lbs chicken breast, cut into cubes
- 1 cup fresh blueberries
- ¼ cup balsamic vinegar
- 2 tbsp honey
- 1 tbsp olive oil
- 1 tsp garlic powder
- Salt and pepper, to taste

Instructions:

1. In a blender, combine blueberries, balsamic vinegar, honey, olive oil, garlic powder, salt, and pepper. Blend until smooth.
2. Thread the chicken onto skewers and brush with the blueberry BBQ sauce.
3. Grill the skewers over medium heat for 5-7 minutes per side, or until the chicken is cooked through.
4. Serve the skewers with extra blueberry BBQ sauce on the side.

Raspberry Rose Sorbet

Ingredients:

- 2 cups fresh raspberries
- ¾ cup sugar
- 1 tbsp lemon juice
- 1 tsp rose water
- 1 cup water

Instructions:

1. In a blender, combine raspberries, sugar, lemon juice, rose water, and water. Blend until smooth.
2. Strain the mixture through a fine-mesh sieve to remove seeds.
3. Pour the strained mixture into an ice cream maker and churn according to the manufacturer's instructions.
4. Transfer the sorbet to a container and freeze for at least 2 hours before serving.

Blackberry Lemon Curd Tartlets

Ingredients:

- 1 pre-made tartlet crust (or homemade)
- 1 cup blackberries
- 1 cup sugar
- 3 large eggs
- ½ cup fresh lemon juice
- 2 tbsp lemon zest
- 6 tbsp unsalted butter, cubed

Instructions:

1. Preheat the oven to 350°F (175°C) and bake the tartlet crusts according to package instructions.
2. In a small saucepan, combine blackberries and sugar over medium heat. Stir until the berries break down and release their juice.
3. In a bowl, whisk eggs, lemon juice, and lemon zest. Slowly whisk in the blackberry mixture.
4. Pour the mixture back into the saucepan and cook over low heat, stirring constantly, until it thickens.
5. Remove from heat and stir in butter until smooth.
6. Fill the cooled tartlet crusts with the lemon curd mixture and refrigerate for at least 2 hours before serving.

Mixed Berry Spinach Salad

Ingredients:

- 4 cups fresh spinach
- 1 cup strawberries, sliced
- ½ cup blueberries
- ½ cup raspberries
- ¼ cup sliced almonds
- ¼ cup crumbled feta cheese
- ¼ cup balsamic vinaigrette

Instructions:

1. In a large salad bowl, combine the spinach, strawberries, blueberries, and raspberries.
2. Top with sliced almonds and crumbled feta cheese.
3. Drizzle with balsamic vinaigrette and toss to combine. Serve immediately.

Cranberry Apple Stuffing

Ingredients:

- 1 loaf of bread, cubed
- 1 apple, chopped
- 1 cup fresh cranberries
- 1 small onion, chopped
- 2 celery stalks, chopped
- 2 tbsp unsalted butter
- 1 cup chicken broth
- 1 tsp dried sage
- 1 tsp thyme
- Salt and pepper, to taste

Instructions:

1. Preheat the oven to 350°F (175°C).
2. In a large skillet, melt butter over medium heat. Sauté onion, celery, and apple until softened, about 5 minutes.
3. Add cranberries, sage, thyme, salt, and pepper. Cook for an additional 2 minutes.
4. In a large bowl, combine the bread cubes and the sautéed mixture. Slowly add chicken broth, stirring until the bread is moistened.
5. Transfer the mixture to a greased baking dish and cover with foil. Bake for 30 minutes.
6. Remove foil and bake for another 15 minutes, or until the top is golden.

Strawberry Chocolate Chip Cookies

Ingredients:

- 1 ½ cups all-purpose flour
- ½ tsp baking soda
- ¼ tsp salt
- ½ cup unsalted butter, softened
- ¾ cup sugar
- 1 large egg
- 1 tsp vanilla extract
- 1 cup fresh strawberries, diced
- ½ cup mini chocolate chips

Instructions:

1. Preheat your oven to 350°F (175°C).
2. In a small bowl, whisk together flour, baking soda, and salt.
3. In a large bowl, cream together butter and sugar until light and fluffy.
4. Beat in the egg and vanilla extract. Gradually add the dry ingredients, mixing until combined.
5. Gently fold in the strawberries and chocolate chips.
6. Drop spoonfuls of dough onto a baking sheet, spacing them 2 inches apart.
7. Bake for 12-15 minutes, or until the edges are golden. Cool on a wire rack.

Blueberry Honey Glazed Pork Chops

Ingredients:

- 4 bone-in pork chops
- 1 cup fresh blueberries
- 2 tbsp honey
- 2 tbsp balsamic vinegar
- 1 tbsp olive oil
- Salt and pepper, to taste

Instructions:

1. Season the pork chops with salt and pepper.
2. In a skillet, heat olive oil over medium-high heat. Cook the pork chops for 4-5 minutes per side, until browned and cooked through.
3. In a small saucepan, combine blueberries, honey, and balsamic vinegar. Simmer for 5-7 minutes, or until the blueberries burst and the sauce thickens.
4. Drizzle the blueberry glaze over the cooked pork chops and serve immediately.

Raspberry Swirl Ice Cream

Ingredients:

- 2 cups heavy cream
- 1 cup whole milk
- ¾ cup sugar
- 1 tsp vanilla extract
- 1 cup fresh raspberries
- 2 tbsp sugar (for raspberries)

Instructions:

1. In a large bowl, whisk together cream, milk, sugar, and vanilla extract until the sugar dissolves.
2. Pour the mixture into an ice cream maker and churn according to the manufacturer's instructions.
3. In a separate bowl, mash the raspberries with 2 tbsp sugar.
4. Once the ice cream is churned, swirl the raspberry puree through the ice cream.
5. Freeze for at least 4 hours before serving.

Blackberry Sage Gravy

Ingredients:

- 1 cup fresh blackberries
- 2 tbsp unsalted butter
- 2 tbsp all-purpose flour
- 1 cup chicken broth
- ½ tsp dried sage
- Salt and pepper, to taste

Instructions:

1. In a small saucepan, melt butter over medium heat. Add flour and cook for 1-2 minutes to form a roux.
2. Gradually whisk in chicken broth and cook until the sauce thickens, about 5-7 minutes.
3. Stir in blackberries, sage, salt, and pepper. Simmer for an additional 5 minutes until the berries break down.
4. Serve over roasted meats or mashed potatoes.

Mixed Berry Pavlova

Ingredients:

- 4 large egg whites
- 1 cup granulated sugar
- 1 tsp vanilla extract
- 1 tsp cornstarch
- 1 tsp white vinegar
- 2 cups mixed berries (strawberries, blueberries, raspberries)
- 1 cup heavy cream
- 2 tbsp powdered sugar

Instructions:

1. Preheat your oven to 250°F (120°C). Line a baking sheet with parchment paper.
2. In a large bowl, beat egg whites until soft peaks form. Gradually add sugar, 1 tbsp at a time, and continue to beat until stiff peaks form.
3. Fold in vanilla extract, cornstarch, and vinegar.
4. Spoon the meringue onto the parchment paper, shaping it into a circular base.
5. Bake for 1 hour, then turn off the oven and let the meringue cool completely.
6. Whip the cream with powdered sugar until soft peaks form.
7. Once the pavlova has cooled, top it with whipped cream and mixed berries. Serve immediately.

Cranberry Ginger Cocktail

Ingredients:

- 1 cup cranberry juice
- ½ cup ginger beer
- 1 tbsp fresh lime juice
- 1 oz vodka (optional)
- Ice
- Fresh cranberries and mint for garnish

Instructions:

1. In a cocktail shaker, combine cranberry juice, ginger beer, lime juice, and vodka (if using).
2. Shake well to combine.
3. Pour over ice into a glass.
4. Garnish with fresh cranberries and a sprig of mint.
5. Serve immediately and enjoy this refreshing cocktail.

Strawberry Ricotta Pancakes

Ingredients:

- 1 cup all-purpose flour
- 1 tbsp sugar
- 1 tsp baking powder
- ½ tsp salt
- 1 cup ricotta cheese
- 2 large eggs
- ½ cup milk
- 1 tsp vanilla extract
- 1 cup fresh strawberries, chopped
- Butter or oil for cooking

Instructions:

1. In a large bowl, whisk together flour, sugar, baking powder, and salt.
2. In another bowl, combine ricotta, eggs, milk, and vanilla extract.
3. Add the wet ingredients to the dry ingredients and mix until just combined.
4. Gently fold in chopped strawberries.
5. Heat a skillet over medium heat and add a little butter or oil.
6. Pour ¼ cup of batter for each pancake onto the skillet and cook until bubbles form on the surface, then flip and cook until golden brown.
7. Serve with extra strawberries and syrup.

Blueberry Lemon Yogurt Cake

Ingredients:

- 1 ½ cups all-purpose flour
- 1 tsp baking powder
- ½ tsp baking soda
- ¼ tsp salt
- 1 cup Greek yogurt
- 1 cup sugar
- 3 large eggs
- 1 tsp vanilla extract
- 1 tbsp lemon zest
- ½ cup fresh blueberries

Instructions:

1. Preheat your oven to 350°F (175°C) and grease a loaf pan.
2. In a medium bowl, whisk together flour, baking powder, baking soda, and salt.
3. In a large bowl, beat together yogurt, sugar, eggs, vanilla, and lemon zest until smooth.
4. Gradually add the dry ingredients to the wet mixture and stir until combined.
5. Gently fold in the blueberries.
6. Pour the batter into the prepared pan and bake for 50-60 minutes, or until a toothpick comes out clean.
7. Cool before slicing and serving.

Raspberry Almond Crumb Bars

Ingredients:

- 1 ½ cups all-purpose flour
- ¾ cup granulated sugar
- ½ tsp baking powder
- ¼ tsp salt
- ¾ cup unsalted butter, softened
- 1 egg
- 1 tsp vanilla extract
- 1 cup fresh raspberries
- ½ cup sliced almonds

Instructions:

1. Preheat your oven to 350°F (175°C). Grease an 8x8-inch baking pan.
2. In a bowl, mix together flour, sugar, baking powder, and salt.
3. Cut in the butter until the mixture resembles coarse crumbs.
4. Add the egg and vanilla extract and stir until combined.
5. Press about ⅔ of the dough into the bottom of the prepared pan.
6. Spread the raspberries evenly over the dough, then sprinkle with sliced almonds.
7. Crumble the remaining dough over the top.
8. Bake for 30-35 minutes or until golden.
9. Let cool before cutting into bars.

Blackberry Jalapeño Jam

Ingredients:

- 2 cups fresh blackberries
- 1 cup sugar
- 1 tbsp fresh lime juice
- 1-2 jalapeños, seeded and finely chopped
- 1 packet fruit pectin (or follow package instructions)

Instructions:

1. In a medium saucepan, combine blackberries, sugar, lime juice, and jalapeños.
2. Bring the mixture to a simmer over medium heat and cook for 10 minutes, mashing the berries as they cook.
3. Add the fruit pectin and stir to combine.
4. Bring to a boil and cook for 5 minutes, stirring frequently.
5. Remove from heat and let cool for 5 minutes before pouring into sterilized jars.
6. Seal and store in the refrigerator for up to 2 weeks.

Mixed Berry Oat Bars

Ingredients:

- 1 ½ cups rolled oats
- 1 cup flour
- ½ tsp baking powder
- ¼ tsp salt
- ½ cup honey
- 1/3 cup unsweetened applesauce
- 2 cups mixed berries (strawberries, raspberries, blueberries)

Instructions:

1. Preheat your oven to 350°F (175°C) and grease an 8x8-inch baking pan.
2. In a large bowl, combine oats, flour, baking powder, and salt.
3. Stir in honey and applesauce until the mixture is well combined.
4. Gently fold in the mixed berries.
5. Press the mixture evenly into the prepared pan.
6. Bake for 25-30 minutes, or until the bars are golden brown.
7. Let cool completely before cutting into bars.

Cranberry Bourbon Glazed Ham

Ingredients:

- 1 boneless ham (about 4 lbs)
- 1 cup cranberry sauce
- 1/4 cup bourbon
- 1/4 cup brown sugar
- 1 tbsp Dijon mustard
- 1/4 tsp ground cloves

Instructions:

1. Preheat your oven to 350°F (175°C).
2. Score the surface of the ham in a diamond pattern and place it in a roasting pan.
3. In a saucepan, combine cranberry sauce, bourbon, brown sugar, mustard, and cloves.
4. Simmer over low heat for 10-15 minutes, stirring occasionally.
5. Brush the glaze over the ham and bake for 1-1½ hours, basting with the glaze every 20 minutes.
6. Let the ham rest before slicing and serving.

Strawberry Kiwi Popsicles

Ingredients:

- 1 cup fresh strawberries, hulled
- 1 cup fresh kiwi, peeled and chopped
- 2 tbsp honey or sweetener of choice
- 1/2 cup coconut water or juice

Instructions:

1. In a blender, combine strawberries, kiwi, honey, and coconut water.
2. Blend until smooth.
3. Pour the mixture into popsicle molds and freeze for 4-6 hours, or until fully frozen.
4. Remove from molds and serve as a refreshing summer treat.

Blueberry Balsamic Chicken Salad

Ingredients:

- 2 chicken breasts, cooked and shredded
- 2 cups mixed greens
- 1 cup fresh blueberries
- 1/4 cup crumbled feta cheese
- 1/4 cup balsamic vinaigrette
- 1 tbsp olive oil
- Salt and pepper, to taste

Instructions:

1. In a large bowl, toss the chicken, mixed greens, blueberries, and feta cheese together.
2. Drizzle with balsamic vinaigrette and olive oil.
3. Toss to combine and season with salt and pepper.
4. Serve immediately as a light and refreshing salad.

Raspberry Chocolate Lava Cakes

Ingredients:

- 4 oz semi-sweet chocolate, chopped
- ½ cup unsalted butter
- 2 large eggs
- 2 large egg yolks
- ½ cup powdered sugar
- ¼ cup all-purpose flour
- ½ tsp vanilla extract
- ½ cup fresh raspberries

Instructions:

1. Preheat your oven to 425°F (220°C). Grease two ramekins and dust with cocoa powder.
2. In a microwave-safe bowl, melt the chocolate and butter together until smooth.
3. In a separate bowl, whisk together eggs, egg yolks, powdered sugar, and vanilla extract.
4. Fold in the melted chocolate mixture, then sift in the flour and stir until just combined.
5. Pour the batter into the ramekins, then drop a few raspberries into the center of each.
6. Bake for 12-14 minutes until the edges are set but the center is soft.
7. Allow to cool for a few minutes before inverting onto plates. Serve warm.

Blackberry Vanilla Bean Panna Cotta

Ingredients:

- 1 ½ cups heavy cream
- ½ cup whole milk
- ¼ cup granulated sugar
- 1 vanilla bean, split and scraped (or 1 tsp vanilla extract)
- 1 packet gelatin
- 2 tbsp water
- 1 cup fresh blackberries
- 1 tbsp honey

Instructions:

1. In a saucepan, combine cream, milk, sugar, and the vanilla bean (or extract). Heat over medium until it begins to simmer.
2. Meanwhile, dissolve the gelatin in 2 tbsp of cold water and let sit for 5 minutes.
3. Stir the gelatin into the warm cream mixture until fully dissolved. Remove from heat and strain to remove the vanilla pod.
4. Pour the mixture into individual serving glasses and refrigerate for at least 4 hours, or overnight.
5. For the topping, mash the blackberries with honey and spoon over the panna cotta before serving.

Mixed Berry Quinoa Salad

Ingredients:

- 1 cup cooked quinoa
- 1 cup fresh strawberries, chopped
- 1 cup fresh blueberries
- 1 cup fresh raspberries
- ¼ cup chopped fresh mint
- ¼ cup honey
- 2 tbsp fresh lime juice

Instructions:

1. In a large bowl, combine cooked quinoa, strawberries, blueberries, raspberries, and mint.
2. In a small bowl, whisk together honey and lime juice.
3. Drizzle the dressing over the salad and toss gently to combine.
4. Serve chilled as a refreshing and nutrient-packed side dish or light meal.

Cranberry Almond Energy Balls

Ingredients:

- 1 cup rolled oats
- ½ cup dried cranberries
- ½ cup almond butter
- ¼ cup honey
- 1 tsp vanilla extract
- ¼ cup ground flaxseed
- 2 tbsp almond meal
- Pinch of salt

Instructions:

1. In a bowl, combine oats, cranberries, flaxseed, almond meal, and salt.
2. Stir in almond butter, honey, and vanilla extract until well combined.
3. Roll the mixture into small balls, about 1 inch in diameter.
4. Chill in the refrigerator for at least 30 minutes before serving.
5. Store in an airtight container in the fridge for up to 1 week.

Strawberry Lavender Mocktail

Ingredients:

- 1 cup fresh strawberries, hulled
- 1 tsp dried lavender
- 1 tbsp honey
- 1 tbsp fresh lemon juice
- 1 cup sparkling water
- Ice cubes
- Fresh strawberries and lavender sprigs for garnish

Instructions:

1. In a small saucepan, combine strawberries, lavender, and honey with 1 cup of water. Simmer for 5-7 minutes, then strain the mixture into a glass.
2. Add lemon juice to the strawberry lavender syrup.
3. Fill a glass with ice and pour the syrup over it.
4. Top with sparkling water and garnish with fresh strawberries and lavender.
5. Serve chilled for a refreshing, floral mocktail.

Blueberry Coconut Ice Cream

Ingredients:

- 2 cups fresh blueberries
- 1 cup coconut milk
- ½ cup sugar
- 1 tsp vanilla extract
- Pinch of salt

Instructions:

1. Blend the blueberries, coconut milk, sugar, vanilla extract, and salt until smooth.
2. Pour the mixture into an ice cream maker and churn according to the manufacturer's instructions.
3. Transfer the ice cream to a container and freeze for at least 4 hours or until firm.
4. Serve and enjoy a creamy, dairy-free ice cream.

Raspberry Hazelnut Tart

Ingredients:

- 1 tart crust (store-bought or homemade)
- 1 cup fresh raspberries
- ½ cup hazelnuts, toasted and chopped
- ½ cup dark chocolate chips
- ¼ cup heavy cream
- 2 tbsp honey

Instructions:

1. Preheat your oven to 350°F (175°C).
2. Bake the tart crust according to package directions and let it cool.
3. In a saucepan, heat the cream and honey until warm, then pour over the chocolate chips. Stir until smooth to create the ganache.
4. Pour the ganache into the cooled tart crust and smooth the top.
5. Decorate with fresh raspberries and chopped hazelnuts.
6. Refrigerate for at least 1 hour before serving.

Blackberry Thyme Roasted Vegetables

Ingredients:

- 2 cups fresh blackberries
- 2 cups mixed vegetables (carrots, zucchini, bell peppers, etc.)
- 2 tbsp olive oil
- 1 tsp fresh thyme leaves
- Salt and pepper to taste

Instructions:

1. Preheat your oven to 400°F (200°C).
2. Toss the mixed vegetables with olive oil, thyme, salt, and pepper.
3. Spread the vegetables evenly on a baking sheet and roast for 20-25 minutes until tender.
4. In the last 5 minutes of roasting, add the blackberries to the pan.
5. Serve the roasted vegetables with a drizzle of olive oil and extra thyme for flavor.

Mixed Berry Breakfast Parfait

Ingredients:

- 2 cups mixed berries (strawberries, blueberries, raspberries)
- 2 cups Greek yogurt
- ¼ cup honey
- 1 cup granola

Instructions:

1. In a glass or jar, layer Greek yogurt, honey, mixed berries, and granola.
2. Repeat the layers until the jar is full.
3. Top with additional fresh berries and a drizzle of honey.
4. Serve immediately or refrigerate for a few hours for a grab-and-go breakfast.

Cranberry Glazed Meatballs

Ingredients:

- 1 lb ground beef or turkey
- ½ cup breadcrumbs
- 1 egg
- 1 tsp garlic powder
- 1 tsp onion powder
- Salt and pepper to taste
- 1 cup cranberry sauce
- 2 tbsp brown sugar
- 1 tbsp balsamic vinegar
- 1 tbsp Dijon mustard

Instructions:

1. Preheat your oven to 375°F (190°C).
2. In a bowl, mix ground meat, breadcrumbs, egg, garlic powder, onion powder, salt, and pepper.
3. Form the mixture into 1-inch meatballs and place them on a baking sheet lined with parchment paper.
4. Bake for 15-20 minutes, or until cooked through.
5. In a saucepan, combine cranberry sauce, brown sugar, balsamic vinegar, and Dijon mustard. Simmer over medium heat for 5-7 minutes until the sauce thickens.
6. Toss the baked meatballs in the cranberry glaze and serve.

Strawberry Rosewater Macarons

Ingredients:

- 1 cup powdered sugar
- ½ cup almond flour
- 2 large egg whites
- ¼ cup granulated sugar
- ½ tsp rosewater
- ½ cup fresh strawberries, pureed
- 1 cup unsalted butter, softened
- 2 cups powdered sugar (for filling)

Instructions:

1. Preheat your oven to 300°F (150°C).
2. In a food processor, blend powdered sugar and almond flour, then sift to remove any lumps.
3. Whisk egg whites until stiff peaks form, then gradually add granulated sugar.
4. Gently fold the dry ingredients into the egg whites.
5. Transfer the batter into a piping bag and pipe small rounds onto a baking sheet.
6. Let the macarons rest for 30 minutes, then bake for 15-18 minutes.
7. For the filling, beat butter, powdered sugar, and rosewater until smooth. Add strawberry puree and mix well.
8. Once the macarons have cooled, sandwich them together with the strawberry rosewater filling.

Blueberry Lemonade

Ingredients:

- 1 cup fresh blueberries
- 2 cups water
- ½ cup lemon juice
- ¼ cup sugar (adjust to taste)
- Ice cubes
- Lemon slices and mint for garnish

Instructions:

1. In a saucepan, combine blueberries, water, and sugar. Simmer over medium heat for 5-7 minutes, mashing the berries as they cook.
2. Strain the mixture through a fine mesh sieve to remove the solids.
3. Stir in the lemon juice and refrigerate until chilled.
4. Serve over ice, garnished with lemon slices and fresh mint.

Raspberry Brie Puff Pastry

Ingredients:

- 1 sheet puff pastry, thawed
- 1 cup fresh raspberries
- 8 oz brie cheese, cut into small pieces
- 2 tbsp honey
- 1 egg (for egg wash)

Instructions:

1. Preheat your oven to 375°F (190°C).
2. Roll out the puff pastry on a floured surface.
3. Place brie cheese in the center, then top with raspberries and drizzle with honey.
4. Fold the edges of the pastry over the filling to form a parcel.
5. Brush the pastry with the egg wash and bake for 25-30 minutes, or until golden brown.
6. Let cool slightly before slicing and serving.

Blackberry Bourbon Smash

Ingredients:

- 1 cup fresh blackberries
- 2 oz bourbon
- 1 oz simple syrup
- ½ oz fresh lemon juice
- 5-6 mint leaves
- Ice cubes
- Club soda (optional)

Instructions:

1. Muddle blackberries, mint leaves, and lemon juice in a shaker.
2. Add bourbon and simple syrup, then fill the shaker with ice.
3. Shake vigorously for about 10 seconds.
4. Strain into a glass filled with ice and top with club soda, if desired.
5. Garnish with additional blackberries and mint leaves.

Mixed Berry Cobbler

Ingredients:

- 2 cups mixed berries (strawberries, blueberries, raspberries)
- ¼ cup granulated sugar
- 1 tbsp cornstarch
- 1 tsp lemon juice
- 1 cup all-purpose flour
- 1 tsp baking powder
- ¼ tsp salt
- 6 tbsp unsalted butter, cubed
- ½ cup buttermilk
- ¼ cup granulated sugar (for topping)

Instructions:

1. Preheat your oven to 375°F (190°C).
2. In a bowl, mix berries, ¼ cup sugar, cornstarch, and lemon juice. Transfer the berry mixture to a greased 9x9 baking dish.
3. In another bowl, whisk together flour, baking powder, and salt. Add cubed butter and cut it into the flour mixture until it resembles coarse crumbs.
4. Pour in the buttermilk and stir until just combined.
5. Drop spoonfuls of the biscuit dough over the berry mixture. Sprinkle the remaining sugar on top.
6. Bake for 35-40 minutes, or until the topping is golden and the berries are bubbly.
7. Let cool for a few minutes before serving.

Cranberry Chocolate Bark

Ingredients:

- 8 oz dark chocolate, chopped
- ½ cup dried cranberries
- ¼ cup roasted almonds, chopped
- 2 tbsp white chocolate, melted (optional)

Instructions:

1. Line a baking sheet with parchment paper.
2. Melt the dark chocolate in a heatproof bowl over a pot of simmering water or in the microwave in 30-second intervals, stirring between.
3. Pour the melted chocolate onto the prepared baking sheet and spread it evenly.
4. Sprinkle dried cranberries and chopped almonds over the chocolate.
5. Drizzle with melted white chocolate for an elegant touch.
6. Refrigerate for at least 1 hour, or until the chocolate is firm.
7. Break into pieces and serve.

Strawberry Mango Salsa

Ingredients:

- 1 cup fresh strawberries, diced
- 1 cup mango, diced
- ¼ cup red onion, finely chopped
- 1 small jalapeño, seeded and finely chopped
- 2 tbsp fresh cilantro, chopped
- 1 tbsp fresh lime juice
- Salt and pepper to taste

Instructions:

1. In a medium bowl, combine strawberries, mango, red onion, jalapeño, and cilantro.
2. Add lime juice and mix well.
3. Season with salt and pepper to taste.
4. Serve immediately with tortilla chips or as a topping for grilled chicken or fish.

Blueberry Protein Pancakes

Ingredients:

- 1 cup rolled oats
- 1 cup cottage cheese
- 4 large eggs
- 1 tsp vanilla extract
- ½ tsp baking powder
- ½ cup blueberries
- 1 tbsp honey (optional)

Instructions:

1. Blend oats, cottage cheese, eggs, vanilla extract, and baking powder in a blender until smooth.
2. Heat a non-stick pan or griddle over medium heat and lightly grease with cooking spray.
3. Pour ¼ cup of batter onto the hot pan for each pancake, adding a few blueberries to the top.
4. Cook for 2-3 minutes on each side, flipping when bubbles form on the surface.
5. Serve with a drizzle of honey and extra blueberries.

Raspberry Lime Mousse

Ingredients:

- 1 ½ cups fresh raspberries
- 1 cup heavy cream
- ½ cup powdered sugar
- 1 tsp lime zest
- 2 tbsp fresh lime juice
- 1 tsp vanilla extract

Instructions:

1. In a blender or food processor, blend raspberries until smooth. Strain through a fine mesh sieve to remove seeds.
2. In a mixing bowl, whip heavy cream with powdered sugar until stiff peaks form.
3. Gently fold raspberry puree, lime zest, lime juice, and vanilla extract into the whipped cream.
4. Spoon the mousse into serving glasses and refrigerate for at least 2 hours.
5. Garnish with additional raspberries and a lime slice before serving.

www.ingramcontent.com/pod-product-compliance
Lightning Source LLC
LaVergne TN
LVHW061950070526
838199LV00060B/4061